GW00994491

E. W. KENYON
Author
(1867-1948)

Identification

A Romance in Redemption

By E. W. KENYON

Twenty-Third Printing

TABLE OF CONTENTS

INTRODUCTION

We are dealing with the almost unknown fact of our Identification with Christ.

At once you ask, "What does Identification mean?"

It means our complete union with Him in His Substitutionary Sacrifice.

For instance, this term is used: "I have been crucified with Christ." This is our Identification with Christ in His Crucifixion.

I died with Christ.

I was buried with Christ.

I suffered with Christ.

I was made alive with Christ.

Now I am seated with Him.

This little preposition "with" is the key that has unlocked a long-hidden truth that is of vital importance to us.

The first two or three chapters of this little book will lead you into the ante-chamber of God's greatest Revelation connected with the New Creation.

Chapter One

THE LAW OF IDENTIFICATION

The teaching of Identification is the legal side of our Redemption.

It unveils to us what God did in Christ for us, from the time He went to the Cross, until He sat down on the right hand of the Father.

The vital side of Redemption is what the Holy Spirit, through the Word, is doing in us now.

Several times Paul uses the preposition "with" in connection with His Substitutionary teaching.

Gal. 2:20 "I have been crucified WITH Christ."

Then he tells us that "he died WITH Christ," that "he was buried WITH Christ."

This gives us the key that unlocks the great teachings of Identification.

Christ became one with us in sin, that we might become one with Him in Righteousness.

He became as we were, to the end that we might be as He is now.

He became one with us in death, that we might be one with Him in life.

There is a two-fold oneness: first His oneness with our sin on the cross; second, our oneness with Him in His glory on the throne.

Eph. 2:6 "And raised us up with him, and made us to sit with him in the heavenly places, in Christ Jesus."

He became as we were, so that we might become as He is.

He died to make us live.

He was made sin to make us Righteous.

He became weak to make us strong.

He suffered shame to give us glory.

He went to Hell in order to take us to Heaven.

He was condemned in order to Justify us.

He was made sick in order that healing might be ours.

He was cast out from the presence of God in order to make us welcome there.

In the fact of Identification we have one of the richest phases of Redemption.

Chapter Two

CRUCIFIED WITH CHRIST

When Paul said, "I have been crucified with Christ," it meant he had been judged, condemned, cast out, stripped naked, and nailed to the cross.

The very thought of crucifixion to a Jew, and especially to a Pharisee, brought a sense of shame and horror.

When Saul of Tarsus identified himself with the Man, Jesus, accepted Him as his Savior, and confessed Him as his Lord, that moment he became a crucified man to the Jewish people.

He became an outcast.

No wonder he said in Gal. 6:14 that the world had been crucified unto him, and he had been crucified unto the world.

The world had been stripped naked to Paul.

There was no longer any delusion in regard to it.

He could no longer be deceived.

He knew its cruelty.

He had felt its lash upon his back.

He remembered the stoning that had left him unconscious.

He remembered that in every place he went, he faced the anger, bitterness, and jealousy of men.

He had been stripped naked to the world.

There was nothing in him that the world desired.

That little Jew, with his mighty message, and his

tremendous power in prayer, had been crucified to the world.

We understand what crucifixion actually means.

Paul saw his Identification with Christ in His crucifixion.

We understand that crucifixion did not mean death.

It meant union with Christ in His disgrace and suffering.

Rom. 6:6 "Knowing this, that our old man was crucified with him, that the body of sin might be done away, that so we should no longer be in bondage to sin.

Crucifixion points the way to death.

In the Spirit's great argument of our Identification with Christ He said that our old man, this hidden man of the heart, our spirit, the real man who was filled with spiritual death, Satanic nature, was nailed to the cross in Christ.

Christ went there, not for Himself, not as a martyr, but as a Substitute.

We were nailed to the cross with Christ.

We were crucified with him.

The object of the crucifixion, in the mind of the mob, was to get rid of this Man whom they hated.

In the mind of Justice it meant His Identification with humanity in its sin and suffering, and our Identification with Him in His crucifixion.

Chapter Three

HE WAS MADE SIN

In the great drama of our Redemption, as soon as Christ was nailed to the cross, with His crown of thorns, and with the howling mob that surrounded Him, Justice began to do its awful work behind the scenes.

Sense-Knowledge men and women who surrounded the cross could only see the physical man, Jesus, hanging there.

God could see His spirit.

Angels could see His spirit.

Demons could see the real man, hidden in that body.

Then came the dreadful hour when 2 Corinthians 5:21 was fulfilled.

"Him who knew no sin he made to be sin on our behalf; that we might become the righteousness of God in him."

Isaiah 53:5 "He was wounded for our transgressions, he was bruised for our iniquities; the chastisement of our peace was upon him; and with his stripes we are healed. All we like sheep have gone astray; we have turned everyone to his own way; and Jehovah hath laid on him the iniquity of us all."

On that awful cross, He not only became sin, but He became a curse, for in Galatians 3:13 it tells us, "Christ redeemed us from the curse of the law, having become a curse for us; for it is written, Cursed is everyone that hangeth on a tree." (The word "us" there refers to the Jews).

He came as a Jew under the First Covenant to redeem all those who were under that Covenant from the curse of the Law.

When He was hanging on the cross, He was not only sin, but He was a curse.

Is it any wonder that God turned His back upon Him?

Is it any wonder He cried in His agony, "My God, my God, why hast thou forsaken me?"

He had taken the sinner's place in Judgment.

All the forces of darkness had overwhelmed Him.

He was our sin Substitute.

Sin was not reckoned to Him. Sin was not set to His account. He became sin.

Our Senses reel under the staggering thought of it.

We cannot grasp it.

Only our spirits can fathom the depths of His agony.

You can hear Paul cry, (Philippians 3:10) "That I may know him, and the power of his resurrection, and the fellowship of his sufferings, becoming conformed unto his death."

Paul's prayer amazes one.

He wanted to share in the death-agonies of Christ.

He wanted to fellowship His sufferings.

But Paul could not do that.

No one could do it.

No angel could do it.

It was God's own work that must be wrought.

When He surrendered His Son to death, He unveiled a love that beggars description.

Chapter Four

HE WAS MADE SICK

The next step in this awful drama is found in Isaiah 53:3-5. (R. V., marg.)

"He was despised, and rejected of men; a man of pains, and acquainted with sickness: and as one from whom men hide their face he was despised; and we esteemed him not. Surely he hath borne our sicknesses, and carried our diseases; yet we did esteem him stricken, smitten of God, and afflicted."

It was not what the Roman soldiers nor the angry mob did. It was what God did.

It shocks us when we realize that He was stricken, smitten of God with our diseases and our sin.

There was laid upon Him the diseases and sicknesses of the human race.

Isaiah 53:10 "Yet it pleased Jehovah to bruise him; he hath made him sick."

He was not only made sin and separated from His Father, until His broken heart cried, "My God, my God, why hast thou forsaken me?" but the diseases of the human race fell upon Him.

Isaiah 52:14 (Margin, Cross-Reference Bible) "Just as many were amazed over Him, and princes on His account shuddered, were astonished and appalled, amazed, frightened. His visage was so marred, unlike to a man, and His form unlike to the sons of man, so deformed was His appearance not to be a man, and His figure no longer resembled a man."

This was spiritual suffering.

This was when the hidden man of the heart became not only sin, but sickness.

This was the spiritual side of the agony of the cross.

This was when our sin and diseases were laid upon His spirit.

His spirit was made sin.

His spirit was made sick.

If the heart could only take it in that He was made sin, and that we were Identified with Him on the cross, then we could grasp the reality of His Substitutionary work.

This truth has been a doctrine instead of a reality to most of us.

He not only laid our sin on Him, but He laid us on Him.

The whole man was involved in this sacrifice—His spirit, Soul, and His body.

We were nailed to the cross with Him and in Him.

Our diseases were part of Him.

When the heart recognizes this, it will be the end of the dominion of disease.

For if He was made sick with our sickness, Satan has no legal right to put diseases upon us, and in the Name of Jesus we can free ourselves from Satan's power.

True, we have mortal bodies, but this mortal body is filled with the life of God.

2 Corinthians 5:4 "That what is mortal may be swallowed up of life."

Romans 6:14 "Sin shall not have dominion over you," or literally, "Sin shall not lord it over you."

Neither shall disease and pain lord it over us.

We see now that if Satan has lost his dominion, he cannot put disease upon us.

We understand that sickness is spiritual. It is manifested in our physical bodies as a disease. The world sees sickness in our bodies, God sees sickness in our spirits. God heals us through the Word.

It is the Word that heals our spirits.

It is the Word that recreates us.

It is the Word that produces faith.

It is the Word that unveils to us what we really are in Christ—New Creations.

It is the Word, then, that brings healing to these sick spirits of ours.

Sickness is a spiritual condition manifested in the physical body.

If He was made sin, and if He put our sin away, we need not be ruled by it.

If He was made sick with our sickness, and if He put our diseases away, we need not be ruled by sickness and disease.

We, with our diseases and sicknesses, were nailed to the cross in Christ.

When we recognize this, we will no longer struggle for faith, for Righteousness, and holiness, because we will know that we were nailed to the cross and died with Him, were buried with Him, suffered with Him, were made alive with Him, were Justified with Him, conquered Satan with Him, were raised with Him, and finally were seated with Him. The whole program of that Substitutionary Sacrifice is made real in us by the Spirit through the Word. All these things are ours now. Ephesians 1:3.

Chapter Five

WE DIED WITH HIM

Jesus died twice on the cross.

I knew this for many years, but I had no scriptural evidence of it.

One day I discovered Isaiah 53:9, the answer to my long search.

"And they made his grave with the wicked, and with a rich man in his deaths."

The word "death" is plural in the Hebrew.

Many of you who have Bibles with marginal renderings will notice it.

That is, Jesus died two deaths on the cross: He died spiritually before He died physically.

In John 10:18 He said that no one could take His life from Him.

He could not be killed; He could not die.

Why? Because His body was not mortal.

Jesus had a body like Adam's before he sinned.

It was a perfect, human body, not Mortal, nor Immortal.

It was a body that could not die until sin had taken possession of His spirit.

In other words, Jesus had to die spiritually before He could die physically.

If Jesus' body had been like yours and mine, then He was not Deity, He was not a Substitute, and He did not die for our sins; He merely died as a martyr.

But, if He had a body like the first man Adam's body, that was not Mortal, not subject to death, (that would mean subject to Satan) then He was Deity.

In our last chapter we saw man nailed to the cross with Christ.

In this we see the human race died with the Crucified One.

Paul says, "If we died with Christ, we believe we shall also live with Him." Romans 6:8 and 2 Timothy 2:11.

In these scriptures we notice we died with Christ when He died.

He was our Substitute.

We were one with Him on the cross.

We were one with Him in His death.

He died under our Judgment, in our stead.

He died because He was made sin.

If we accept Him, there can be no judgment for us.

Isaiah 53:10-12 "Yet it pleased Jehovah to bruise him; he hath made him sick: when thou shalt make his soul an offering for sin, he shall see his seed, he shall prolong his days, and the pleasure of Jehovah shall prosper in his hand. He shall see of the travail of his soul, and shall be satisfied: by the knowledge of himself shall my righteous servant justify many; and he shall bear their iniquities. Therefore will I divide him a portion with the great, and he shall divide the spoil with the strong; because he poured out his soul unto death, and was numbered with the transgressors: yet he bare the sin of many, and made intercession for the transgressors."

That sounds just like the Pauline Revelation, doesn't it?

The Pauline Revelation is an unveiling of what happened from the time that Jesus was made sin on the cross, until He sat down at the right hand of God.

Nowhere else can we find that knowledge.

This is Substitution.

This is absolute Identification.

This is a part of the great Substitutionary truth in prophecy.

He poured out His life into death.

Through that death we were made alive.

It was our sin that slew Him.

It is His Righteousness that gives us life.

He drank the cup of death, that we might drink the cup of life.

In that mighty ministry before He arose from the dead, He destroyed death's lordship.

When death slew Him, it slew itself.

He conquered sin when He allowed it to overcome Him.

He conquered Satan when He let Satan gain the mastery over Him.

He conquered disease when He let disease take possession of Him.

He became one with Satan in spiritual death, to make us one with God in spiritual life.

"Him who knew no sin he made to be sin on our behalf; that we might become the righteousness of God in Him." (2 Corinthians 5:21).

He became one with us in weakness, in sin, in disease, and in spiritual death, that He might make us one with Himself in Righteousness, in perfect health, and fellowship with the Father.

He became death's prisoner in order to set us free.

In the mind of Justice, we died to sin and its dominion when we died with Christ.

"He that hath died is justified from sin." (Romans 6:7).

He is free from the lordship of spiritual death.

There was in God's mind at the Crucifixion, a perfect oneness of Christ with us, and in the Resurrection and New Birth, a perfect oneness of us in Christ.

Just as Jesus conquered death by submitting to it, we in the New Creation conquer Satan by submitting to the Lordship of Jesus.

We and our diseases were laid on Him, and became a part of Him when He was made sin with our sin.

We are healed by becoming partakers of His divine nature.

Disease and sickness do not belong to the New Creation.

It is an abnormal thing in the mind of the Father for a child of God to be sick.

We died with Him.

We died to the dominion of sin.

We died to the dominion of disease.

We died to the dominion of circumstances and habits.

1 Peter 2:24 becomes a reality.

"Who his own self bare our sins in His body upon the tree, that we, having died unto sins, might live unto righteousness; by whose stripes ye were healed."

This is Identification, our utter oneness with Him in sin and Judgment on the cross.

"That we, having died unto sins." His death and our death are identical.

This is not His physical death.

This is spiritual.

He died twice there.

He partook of our spiritual death. We were utterly one with Him in that Judgment.

"That we might live unto Righteousness." Or, that we might partake of His Righteousness as He partook of our sins, that we might be Righteous as He became sin with our sins.

Then the next marvelous statement: "By whose stripes ye were healed."

He not only had our sin nature, but He had our diseases.

He took over our diseases; He put them away when He put sin away.

"By His stripes we are healed."

This is thrilling. As He put our sin and diseases away by becoming sin and disease for us, so we partake of His Righteousness and healing when we accept His work for us.

Christ has died once for all as our Sin Substitute.

He, in judgment, met the demands of Justice for us.

He took them with Him when He went to the place of Substitution, the place of Judgment, the place of suffering.

I am convinced that the Father sees us in Christ as perfect, as the finished work of Christ is perfect.

He saw that our union with Satan was a perfect union.
We were one with the devil.

He laid our spiritual death on Christ.

Ephesians 2:10 "For we are His workmanship, created in Christ Jesus."

That work was wrought by the great master workman, Christ, before He arose from the dead.

The Father sees us now in all our beauty and perfection in Christ.

This beauty is all His own. He made us to please His own heart.

We died to sin once for all in Christ.

We died to Satan's dominion.

We died to the old habits that held us in bondage.

We do not need to die again.

The theory of our dying daily with Christ comes from the old version, "I am crucified," which is an incorrect translation.

The passage in 1 Corinthians 15:31 is speaking of Paul's living in the presence of physical death, the expectation of being thrown to the lions in the arena.

We died once with Christ.

Now we live with Him, we reign with Him.

His perfect Redemption is ours.

His perfect Righteousness is ours.

All He is and did is ours.

All we are is His.

The Father made us one with Himself in Christ.

Chapter Six

WE WERE BURIED WITH HIM

We have seen how He became sin with our sin, how He became our Substitute, bearing our diseases.

We have seen Him under the absolute dominion and power of the adversary on the cross.

We saw Him leave the cross, bearing our diseases and sins away as He was conveyed to our place of confinement.

We can see Satan's gratification.

We can see that great celebration in Hell when Satan brought Jesus, a captive, into the prisonhouse.

Read Acts 2:24, 27, 31-32.

You remember how the Philistines rejoiced over Samson, and with what joy they put out his eyes and bound him in helplessness.

What a gala day it must have been in Hell when He who had raised Lazarus from the dead, had destroyed the power of death and disease, had ruled the winds and the waves, had fed the hungry, cast out demons, and defeated Satan in open combat, was conquered and made one with the devil.

He was made sick.

They could see in Him all the diseases of the ages.

What an hour it must have been.

When the disciples took His body from the cross, embalmed it, and laid it in Joseph's tomb, how little they appreciated what He was going through, and what His sufferings were.

How little the world appreciated where Jesus was and what He was doing.

They laid His body in the tomb, and the Roman Government sealed it and set guards to keep watch to see that the body of Jesus was not stolen.

They had heard Him cry, "My God, my God, why hast thou forsaken me?"

God had forsaken Him whom they loved.

They had lost all hope. They had thought that it was He who was going to redeem Israel.

For three days and three nights the Lamb of God was our Substitute in Hell.

He was there for us.

He had our pains and our diseases, our sins and iniquities.

He was there waiting until the claims of Justice were fully met.

Such an hour had never been, never can be again.

There had to be an adequate meeting of the penalty of the transgressions of the human race, and He met them.

He became one with Satan when He became sin, as we now become one with Him when we are Recreated.

Chapter Seven

HE SUFFERED

He endured all that humanity could suffer. It was Deity suffering for humanity.

The eighty-eighth Psalm reads in the margin of the Cross-Reference Bible: "He laid Him in the lowest pit, the pit of the underworld, in the dark places, in dense darkness."

7th verse, "Thy wrath lieth hard upon me." Thy wrath presseth, thou hast laid thy fury upon me. All thy breakers thou has brought upon me. Thou hast let all thy waves strike me. Thou hast let come all thy breakers upon me.

"I have called upon thee my God, day and night; and thou hearest me not."

3rd verse, "Full of trouble, weighted with evils. Thou hast brought me to Sheol, the kingdom of death. I am become a man without God."

The heart cannot take it in.

The mind stands dumb in the presence of truth like this.

15th verse, "While distracted—I endure, I am brought low, I am turned backward. I have borne thy terrors so that I am distracted—helpless. The outbursts of Thy wrath, thy streams of wrath have cut me off.

"Thou hast removed from me mine acquaintances, Even lover and friend, in the Place of Darkness."

FOUR DIVINE ATTRIBUTES SEEN IN HELL

Then we come to the most remarkable part of the suffering of Christ.

He cried, "Wilt thou show wonders to the dead? Shall they that are deceased arise and praise thee?"

Down there in that awful place, God showed His wonders to the dead.

HIS POWER WAS DISPLAYED

He let them see the awfulness of Sin, and the absolute Justice of God.

HIS LOVE WAS DISPLAYED

More than that, He showed the loving kindness of God. He said, "Shall thy loving kindness be shown in the grave?"

HIS ETERNAL FAITHFULNESS DISPLAYED

"Or thy faithfulness in Destruction? Shall thy wonders be known in the dark?"

HIS RIGHTEOUSNESS DISPLAYED

"And thy righteousness in the land of forgetfulness?"

They saw Jesus, who had been made sin with our sin, made as Righteous as He was before He was made sin.

In seeing Him made Righteous, Satan witnessed the fact that Righteousness was made possible for the human in the New Creation.

Christ was made alive right there in the realm of death. He was called "the firstborn out of death."

God said to Him, "Thou art my Son; this day have I begotten thee."

The hosts of Hell saw Him born out of death. They witnessed the triumph of God, and the glory of our matchless Christ.

Wasn't it good of Him to give us this graphic picture not only of His death and suffering, but of His triumph and glory?

Throughout Eternity, in the archives of the Supreme Court of the Universe, there will be records of the Son's visit to Hell, of Satan's defeat, and of man's legal Redemption.

They saw Him put off from Himself the principalities and the powers.

They saw Him paralyze the death-dealing ability of Satan.

They saw Him conquer the hosts of the Black Leader.

They saw Him strip Satan of the authority and dominion of which he had robbed Adam in the Garden.

They saw Him arise from the dead, a victor.

They knew it was the victory of the New Creation.

They saw us made alive with Him, Justified with Him, Raised with Him, made victors with Him.

Revelation 1:17-18 was His song of victory.

"I am the first and the last, and the Living one and I was dead, and behold, I am alive for evermore; and I have the keys of death and of Hades."

Chapter Eight

MADE ALIVE WITH HIM

Colossians 2:13 "And you, being dead through your trespasses and the uncircumcision of your flesh, you I say, did he make alive together with Him."

Ephesians 2:5 "Even when we were dead through our trespasses, made us alive together with Christ."

This is the heart of Redemption.

Romans 6:5 "For if we have become united with him in the likeness of his death, we shall be also in the likeness of his resurrection."

Here we witness the miracle of the Eternities. It took place in that subterranean prisonhouse of death. Jesus was made alive.

Acts 13:33 "God hath fulfilled the same unto our children, in that he raised up Jesus; as also it is written in the second psalm, Thou art My Son, this day have I begotten thee."

Paul, by the Spirit, gave us Colossians 1:18.

"And he is the head of the body, the church: who is the beginning, THE FIRSTBORN FROM THE DEAD; that in all things he might have the preeminence."

He was dead with our death. He had died twice: spiritually and physically.

1 Peter 3:18 "Because Christ also suffered for sins once, the righteous for the unrighteous, that he might bring us to God; being put to death in the flesh, but made alive in the (or His) spirit."

This was not the Holy Spirit; this was His spirit.

What a transformation must have taken place.

How it must have shaken the foundation of that awful place when they saw Him made alive, break the bonds of spiritual death, and hurl back the forces of death that had overwhelmed Him on the cross.

Now we can understand Ephesians 2:10: "We are his workmanship, created in Christ Jesus."

When were we created? In the mind of Justice it was when Jesus was recreated down there.

That is when the Church was really born of God.

GOD'S FAITH IN HIS SON'S WORK

God is a faith God. He counted the things that were not as though they were.

Down there in Hell He counted us Righteous, counted us alive.

He counted us New Creations. His sons and daughters before the day of Pentecost came and the first contingent of the body of Christ came into being.

He counted the things that were not as though they were, and they became.

The moment we accepted Him as our Savior and Lord, this New Birth is made a reality in us.

Chapter Nine

HE WAS MADE RIGHTEOUS

You noticed in the last chapter that He was made alive, and that we were made alive with Him in the mind of Justice.

That life was the nature of the Father, and when He received that nature He became Righteous once more.

He had been made sin.

The moment that He was made alive, God justified Him.

He was declared Righteous because He had satisfied the claims of Justice. He had met every demand of the Supreme Court of the Universe that was against the human race.

He was made Righteous with the life of God as we are made Righteous in the New Creation.

He was made so Righteous that there was not a trace of the sin and the diseases that had become a part of Him in His awful Judgment.

He was made so Righteous, that He could enter into the presence of the Father with no sense of sin or guilt or inferiority.

When He was made sin He cried, "My God, my God, why hast thou forsaken me?"

When He was made alive God said of Him, "Thou art my Son; this day have I begotten thee."

He stood before the angelic hosts as Righteous, as pure, as though He had never been made sin.

The moment that He was made Righteous, He was the absolute monarch of the Universe.

He was the master of the underworld. He was the master of Satan.

As long as He was spiritually dead, filled with sin, Satan ruled over Him.

But when He was made Righteous, He became the dominant master and ruler of Hell.

If He was made Righteous, then all of us who accept Him as our Savior, confess Him as our Lord, and receive Eternal Life are automatically made Righteous that moment, and can dominate the forces of Hell in His Name.

It is all of grace—not of works. We are His workmanship, created in Christ Jesus.

We are created in Righteousness and holiness of truth. Ephesians 4:24.

The same Eternal Life or nature of God that made Jesus Righteous has been imparted to us in the New Birth.

Was it any wonder that the Spirit said through John, "As He is, so are we in this world?"

Now we can understand 2 Corinthians 5:21 "Him who knew no sin he made to be sin on our behalf; that we might become the righteousness of God in him."

Romans 3:26 "That he might himself be righteous, and the righteousness of him that hath faith in Jesus." (literal trans.)

God became the Righteousness of Jesus, and the moment we accept Christ as Savior, confess Him as our

Lord, and believe that God raised Him from the dead, He becomes our Righteousness.

As God became the Righteousness of Jesus, so He becomes the Righteousness of the New Creation.

As He became the life of Jesus, He becomes the life of the New Creation.

This truth will revolutionize the church when once it grasps it.

Ephesians 2:6 "And raised us up with him, and made us to sit with him in the heavenly places, in Christ Jesus."

This could never have been a part of the Revelation unless you were as Righteous as He was.

Can't you see the utter fearlessness this gives you in the presence of all kinds of diseases, of Satan himself?

Can't you see what boldness it gives when you enter His presence?

The sense of oneness with Him is as real as His sense of oneness was with us when He was made sin and sickness.

Let us arise and take our place as victors, as conquerors.

Let us go out and do the work that Jesus began to do when He was here.

Chapter Ten

HE CONQUERED SATAN

This was the greatest event of the eternities.

The eternal Son was Justified, Made Alive in spirit, and put off from Himself the principalities and the powers, making a show of them openly, triumphing over them in it.

He triumphed over Satan.

He conquered the hosts of Hell.

He stripped Satan of the authority and dominion that he had taken from Adam at the Fall.

You were with Him when that battle took place.

You were Identified with Him.

Just as you were Identified with Him when He was Crucified, when He Died, when He was Buried, when He was Made Alive, when He was Justified, you were with Him in that victory over the adversary.

It was your victory, not His.

He did not need to fight that battle; He did it for you.

When He conquered the adversary and stripped him of his authority, in the mind of the Father it was as though you had done it.

You are Satan's master today, just as Jesus was when He arose from the dead.

Just as Jesus conquered the adversary during His earth walk, you can conquer him today.

It means your mastery over all the works of Satan.

It means that you are expected to do the works that Jesus began.

This was the end of defeat and failure.

This was the beginning of a new era.

It is time that we appreciated what God has done for us in Christ.

It is time that we appreciated what it means to be a member of the body of Christ, that we appreciate the position in which He has placed us and the authority He has given us in the Name of Jesus.

When He defeated Satan, it was our victory.

We are now the Righteous victors.

We are Satan's masters.

We now reign as kings in the realm of life through Jesus Christ, our risen Lord.

Satan cannot lord it over us any longer.

Disease is under our feet.

We are New-Creation sons.

There is no problem of faith.

We are His children; all things are ours.

1 Corinthians 3:21 "All things are yours."

We need not have faith for the things that are ours.

Let us thank Him and go out and enjoy the fullness of this marvelous Redemption.

Chapter Eleven

RAISED WITH HIM

The Resurrection of the Lord Jesus is the proof of Satan's defeat, of man's Redemption, and of God's legal right to make the believer a New Creation.

Ephesians 1:7 stands out with peculiar suggestiveness and comfort.

"In whom we have our redemption through his blood, the remission of our trespasses, according to the riches of his grace."

We have our Redemption. It is not something we have to pray or ask for.

The moment we are Born Again, that moment Redemption is ours.

Satan's dominion over us ends.

Our life of servitude and fear has come to an end.

That Redemption is according to the riches of His grace.

We are free.

In these previous chapters we have had an opportunity to see the wealth and riches of the Father's Grace in His Substitutionary work in Christ.

Ephesians 2:6 "And He raised us up with Him, and He made us to sit with Him in the heavenly places, in Christ Jesus."

We were crucified with Him, died with Him, were buried with Him, suffered with Him, were justified with Him, were made alive with Him, conquered Satan with Him, and were raised together with Him.

That resurrection of Jesus is proof of our victory over the adversary.

It is a proof that cannot be denied. Every person who takes Christ as Savior, in the mind of God is a victor over the adversary.

So few of the Father's children have seen this mighty truth; that our victory was in the victory of Christ.

When Jesus broke the bars of death, having conquered death, Satan, and sin, it was our victory.

Colossians 3:1 "If then ye were raised together with Christ," and we were raised together with Christ.

In the mind of the Father it was our translation out of the kingdom of darkness into the kingdom of the Son of His love.

It was our Redemption.

We had broken Satan's dominion over our body, soul, and spirit in Christ.

But perhaps the greatest message of our perfect victory over the adversary is found in Ephesians 1:19-22:

"And what the exceeding greatness of his ability to us-ward who believe, according to that working of the strength of his might which he wrought in Christ, when he raised him from the dead, and made him to sit at his right hand in the heavenlies far above all rule, and authority, and power, and dominion, and every name that is named, not only in this age, but also in that which is to come: and he put all things in subjection under his feet, and gave him to be head over all things to the church, which is his body, the fullness of him that filleth all in all."

The same ability that wrought in the dead body of Jesus to reanimate it and fill it with Immortality is today in the believer.

We are today more than conquerors because of the life of God that was imparted to us in our New Creation.

It is the ability of God unveiled in that Resurrection that so shook the foundations of Hell, so that today, when the believers know that they were raised together with Christ, they know they are victors in every field and over every circumstance, and they may go on from triumph to triumph.

God has lifted the believer above all rule and authority and power and dominion, not only in this age, but in that which is to come.

He put all things in subjection under the believer's feet.

He gave Christ who is the head of the body to be master over all the forces of the universe.

Jesus gave to the believer a legal right to the use of His Name.

He actually gave him the power of attorney so that in the Name of Jesus every demon and every power should obey that Name, in the lips of the believer.

There isn't anything too hard for God.

God's ability is the ability that He gives to us, so His Resurrection is the proof of our right to reign over Satan and demons.

He was raised because He had conquered Satan in our stead, so that we should no longer live in fear of the unseen forces of darkness.

Chapter Twelve

THE HIGH PRIEST

In Matthew 28:6 the angel said to the women who had come to finish the embalming of Jesus that Lord's Day morning: "Ye seek Jesus who was crucified; He is not here. He is risen. Come, see the place where the Lord lay."

He died a Lamb. He arose the Lord High Priest of the New Creation.

You remember from John 20 that Mary saw Him. When she discovered who He was, she fell at His feet.

He said, "Touch me not; for I am not yet ascended unto the Father: but go unto my brethren, and say to them, I ascend unto my Father and your Father, and my God and your God."

What did He mean?

He meant what we read in Heb. 9:11-12. "But Christ having come a high priest of the good things to come, through the greater and more perfect tabernacle not made with hands, that is to say, not of this creation, nor yet with the blood of goats and calves, but with his own blood entered in once for all into the holy place, having obtained eternal redemption."

As the High Priest, He took His own blood and carried it up to the Heavenly Holy of Holies and there presented it to God.

It was accepted, and that red seal is upon the document of our Redemption.

The blood of Jesus Christ, God's Son, is the eternal witness of His finished work for us, of our legal right to Eternal Life, and sonship with all its privileges.

On the basis of that blood, we are more than conquerors.

Satan has no dominion over us. His dominion is utterly broken.

The tokens of that victory are continually before the Father.

Hebrews 7:22 "By so much also hath Jesus become the surety of a better covenant."

If you are in grave danger, or Satan is pressing hard upon you, you call the Father's attention to your rights that are guaranteed on the ground of that blood.

Revelation 12:11 "And they overcame him because of the blood of the Lamb, and because of the word of their testimony."

You have a legal right to the Name of Jesus that casts out demons and breaks Satan's power.

John 16:23 "If ye shall ask anything of the Father, he will give it you in my name."

All things are possible to you, because you are in the family. You have the perfect protection that the blood guarantees.

Chapter Thirteen

CHRIST SAT DOWN

The climax of Redemption was the seating of the Lord Jesus.

After He had been made sin, after He had paid the penalty of our relationship with Satan, after He had suffered all that Justice demanded of us, then Christ, with us, arose from the dead.

We were raised with Him.

He declared we were seated together with Christ.

Ephesians 2:6 "And raised us up with him, and made us to sit with him in the heavenly places, in Christ Jesus."

This was the highest honor that God had ever conferred upon man.

The Son became a man, identified Himself with the human race, delivered the human race from the authority of Satan, and carried His blood into the Holy of Holies to make the Eternal Redemption.

Then He sat down at the right hand of the Majesty on High.

We have a man seated at God's right hand.

He is our representative. He is there to represent us.

This is the crowning event in Redemption, a man seated at God's right hand, and that man is the head of the new body, the Church.

Is it any wonder he shouts, "Blessed be the God and Father of our Lord Jesus Christ, who hath blessed us with every spiritual blessing in the heavenly places in Christ." (Ephesians 1:3).

Not only are we seated in the highest position in the universe, but we are also blessed with every spiritual blessing that is necessary to maintain our place as members of His glorious body.

In the mind of God, everyone of us is in Christ now. He sees us in Him.

When we go to the throne of Grace in prayer, it is as though Jesus were going there, for we go in His Name.

Colossians 3:3 "For ye died, and your life is hid with Christ in God."

We are hidden from the adversary, but we are visible to the Father.

Hebrews 9:24 "For Christ entered not into a holy place made with hands, like in pattern to the true; but into heaven itself, now to appear before the face of God for us."

He is there at the right hand of the Father as our representative, as our Lord, as our Lover who gave Himself for us.

We can see that our Redemption is a completed, finished thing.

If Christ sat down at God's right hand, it is because the Father accepted Him and accepted what He did for us.

The fact that He is seated there is the seal of our acceptance in the Beloved.

Chapter Fourteen

LIBERATING THE ABILITY OF GOD WITHIN US

The most thrilling thing that I have ever learned about Redemption is the marvelous ability of God that is in the Believer.

We have God's life in us.

"Wherefore if any man is in Christ, he is a new creation: the old things are passed away; behold, they are become new." (2 Corinthians 5:17).

Notice carefully that the believer is a New Creation.

He is created in Christ Jesus.

He is the workmanship of God.

This New Creation has become a reality to him because he has received the life and nature of God.

1 John 5:13 "These things I have written unto you, that ye may know that ye have eternal life, even unto you that believe on the name of the Son of God."

You can see now that you have within you, as you read this, if you are His child, the life and nature of God.

2 Peter 1:4 tells us that we have become partakers of the divine nature.

Whereby he hath granted unto us his precious and exceeding great promises; that through these ye may become partakers of the divine nature, having escaped from the corruption that is in the world by lust."

Jesus emphasizes this by His illustration, "I am the vine, ye are the branches." (John 15:5).

The object of His coming was that we might have life, and have it abundantly.

John 10:10 "I came that they may have life, and may have it abundantly."

You have received Eternal life.

That Eternal Life is the nature of the Father as unveiled in Christ.

As a branch of the vine, the same life that is manifested in the vine is flowing out through you and bearing fruit.

It is the vine's life in you that produces fruitage of love, of faith, and of joy.

YOU HAVE GOD'S WORD ABIDING IN YOU

Colossians 3:16 "Let the word of Christ dwell in you richly."

What is it doing there? It is admonishing, it is educating, it is training, it is correcting, it is building faith and love into your spirit.

Acts 20:32 "Now I commend you to God, and to the word of his grace, which is able to build you up, and to give you the inheritance among all them that are sanctified."

It is the Word that builds you up.

It is the Word that makes you know of your inheritance.

It is the Word that unveils to you your relationship to the Father-God.

It is the Word that makes you know your rights and privileges in Christ.

You remember it was the words of Christ that healed

most of the people who came to Him.

He said they were His Father's words.

The Pauline Revelation is the Father's words about Jesus.

When you say you are a New Creation created in Christ, the Father's words are expressing a fact through your lips.

When you say, "In the Name of Jesus, disease, stop being," you are using the Father's words that He spoke through Jesus' lips.

When you step out into your rights of Righteousness and begin to bear fruit, it will be the same kind of fruit Jesus bore in His earth walk.

Righteousness means the ability to stand in the Father's presence without the sense of guilt or inferiority.

This Righteousness become yours through the finished work of Christ.

Romans 4:25 "Who was delivered up for our trespasses, and was raised for our justification." A literal translation of this verse reads: "Who was delivered up on account of our trespasses, and was raised when we were declared Righteous."

When the life of God is liberated, the ability of God as unveiled in the Word is let loose.

They tell us there is power enough in an atom to propel a great ship across the ocean.

If the power that is invested in the life of God that is in you, and the power that is invested in the Word of God (that Word that spoke a universe into being) were let loose in you, things would happen, wouldn't they?

The object of this little message is to let you know that God wants to be set free in you.

YOU HAVE THE NAME OF JESUS

You have committed to memory these scriptures.

You know John 14:13-14 "Whatsoever ye shall ask (or demand) in my name, that will I do, that the Father may be glorified in the Son. If ye shall ask anything in my name, that will I do."

This is not praying to the Father, nor making a request of Jesus. It is using the Name as Peter used it at the beautiful gate when he set that man free from infantile paralysis.

It is commanding the forces of darkness to become obedient to the authority of the Name of Jesus.

That Name is yours. You may not have taken advantage of it. Jesus gave you the power of attorney to use His Name.

He said, (Matthew 28: 18-19) "All authority hath been given unto me in heaven and on earth. Go ye therefore, and make disciples of all the nations."

The word "disciple" means student, one who learns.

We are to make students of the Word of all nations.

You have the ability to go and do it.

"In my name they shall cast out demons . . . they shall lay hands on the sick, and they shall recover. (Mark 16:17-18).

That belongs to you now.

The age of miracles is your age. It is the present age.
You can live and walk in the fulness of God's ability.
You can let that ability loose in you, if you will.

This is love's challenge to let the life of God loose in you, to let the Word loose in you, to give the Name its real place in your life.

YOU HAVE THE HOLY SPIRIT IN YOU

Jesus promised the disciples that the Holy Spirit, who was with them, should be in them.

On the day of Pentecost, after He had recreated them, He entered into their bodies.

What a miracle it is to have God in us.

It is wonderful to have His Word abiding in us when we realize that the universe has been created by His Word, and we have that creative ability in us.

Now we have God Himself in us, along with His Word.

No wonder He said in 1 John 4:4: "Ye are of God, my little children, and have overcome them: because greater is he that is in you than he that is in the world."

The God in us is the same God who spoke a universe into being. The same God is in us who walked the sea in Galilee.

The same God is in us who arose from the dead.

Philippians 2:13 "For it is God who is at work within you."

We have not taken advantage of the riches of grace that belong to us.

How few of us have let God loose in us.

I can feel Him struggling to have His place and to have His rights in the individual members of the body of Christ.

How He longs to heal the sick, to break the power of Satan over the lives of men through us.

Let us let Him loose in us.

YOU HAVE THE RIGHTEOUSNESS OF GOD

We are the Righteousness of God in Christ.

2 Corinthians 5:21 "Him who knew no sin he made to be sin on our behalf; that we might become the righteousness of God in Christ."

Now He wants us to bear the fruit of Righteousness.

2 Corinthians 9:10 "And increase the fruits of your righteousness."

Righteousness is the ability to stand in the Father's presence without condemnation.

It gives us the legal right to the use of the Name of Jesus.

It gives us ability to stand in the presence of diseases of all kinds without fear, in the presence of Satan as an absolute master.

1 John 2:29 "Everyone that doeth righteousness is begotten of God." How few of us have ever done Righteousness.

We have thought it meant only conduct, a carefulness in our walk.

That is implied, but that is not "doing Righteousness."

Doing Righteousness is doing the works that Jesus

wrought, for we are taking Jesus' place.

Righteousness gives us the ability to stand in the presence of God anytime and to stand in the presence of Satan as absolute victors.

How little this has been understood. How little we have majored it.

Now God is waiting for us to bring this truth to the front. He wants us to begin to live Righteousness, to practice Righteousness, to break Satan's dominion, to speak with authority just as Jesus did.

YOU HAVE GOD'S WISDOM

You might say this is the summation of all.

If you have God's ability, God's wisdom, and you let them loose, what limitlessness there will be to your ministry.

It is not a problem of education, but of letting God loose in you, liberating the ability of God that is within you.

Locked up in you today is the ability of God.

Jesus has been made wisdom unto you.

"But of him are ye in Christ Jesus, who was made unto us wisdom from God."

James told the babes in Christ that if they lacked wisdom they could ask for it of God.

James 1:5-8 (Weymouth) "And if any one of you is deficient in wisdom, let him ask God for it, who gives with open hand to all men, and without upbraiding; and it will be given him. But let him ask in faith and have no doubt; for he who has doubts is like the surge of the sea, driven by the wind and tossed into spray. A person of that sort must not expect to receive anything from the Lord—such a one is a man of two minds, undecided in every step he takes."

You are grown up now. You have passed the period of babyhood and now you know that Jesus is your wisdom.

Wisdom is the ability to use knowledge.

You have the knowledge of the life of God that is in you.

You have the knowledge of the power and authority of the Word.

You have the knowledge of your legal right to use the Name of Jesus in your combat with spiritual forces.

You have the knowledge of the fact that God is actually in your body.

Now you are going to use these mighty facts to bless humanity.

LETTING GOD LOOSE IN US

The imprisoned God at last is set free with the Bill of Rights to use us as He pleases.

We are no longer hidden.

People know who we are.

There is a path worn to our cottage, no matter where we live, for we have let God loose in us and have given Him His liberty to heal the sick, to bless the world.

Chapter Fifteen

SATANIC PERSECUTION OF THE RIGHTEOUS

Jesus said, "Blessed are they that have been persecuted for righteousness' sake."

Later He said, "Blessed are ye when men shall reproach and persecute you."

Men do not persecute us for Righteousness' sake.

Satan persecutes us for Righteousness' sake.

Satan fears Righteousness more than any other thing.

On the ground of what God did in Christ for us, when we are Born again, we become the Righteousness of God.

That means that we have the ability to cast out demons, to break the power of Satan, to heal the sick, and to raise the dead.

Righteousness gives deliverance from the fear of Satan and his works.

It gives a new sense of sonship. This son consciousness begets a heroic faith.

It takes away the sense of spiritual inferiority, and utterly destroys sin consciousness in us.

We can walk before men just as Jesus did, because we know that we are New Creations. The old life has been utterly destroyed.

We know that every sin we ever committed has been remitted.

We know that the sins that we committed since we were Born Again, ignorantly or otherwise, have been forgiven, and we stand in the presence of God just as Jesus did when He walked the earth

Dare we take our stand and make this confession boldly?

Satan seeks to keep us sin conscious and to rob us of our son consciousness.

As long as he can keep us sin conscious we are whipped.

Almost all of the teaching today tends to keep the people under condemnation.

The ministry has never realized that its work is to free man from sin consciousness and make him God conscious, son conscious, victor conscious, faith conscious, love conscious.

When we realize that we have been born of love and that we have the love nature of God in us, we will begin to show forth the fragrance of heaven.

Romans 8:37 "Nay, in all these things we are more than conquerors."

When we become victory conscious, we will arise as a strong man out of sleep and take our place among the victors.

The Son has made us free. Let us stand fast in the liberty wherewith His Redemption has set us free.

Chapter Sixteen

KNOWLEDGE OF HIS WILL

This is a problem that bothers most of God's people: how to know the will of the Father.

The will of the Father is wrapped up in the Word. Jesus said, "I came down from heaven not to do mine own will, but the will of Him that sent me."

Jesus knew what the Father's will was. He said, "I always do the things that are pleasing in His sight."

Paul said in 2 Cor. 5: that he made it his business to be well pleasing to the Father.

If Jesus could please the Father and do His will, if Paul could please the Father, know His will and do it, then it is possible for us to do it.

What are the grounds for assurance? In the first place we have His mind and His will in the Word.

If we search the Word diligently, allowing the Spirit to guide us in it, we will arrive in spiritual growth and development through constant meditations in the Word so that His will will be an unconscious consciousness in us.

He said, "Let the Word of Christ dwell in you richly, admonishing you, building you up."

Paul said to the Ephesian church when he bade them goodbye, "I commend you to the Word of His Grace which is able to build you up and give you the inheritance among them that are sanctified."

Col. 1:9, "For this cause also since the day we heard, do not cease to pray and make request for you, that you may be filled with the knowledge of His will in all spiritual wisdom and understanding, to walk worthily of the Lord unto all pleasing, bearing fruit in every good work, and increasing in the knowledge of God."

The word "knowledge" comes from the Greek word "epignosis" which means correct knowledge, full, complete knowledge. We are to be filled with correct knowledge and then He gives us wisdom to use this perfect knowledge.

Someone says, "It does not seem credible that we could have perfect knowledge." Why shouldn't we? We have a perfect Revelation of His will.

The Bible is a perfect book. The Holy Spirit is a perfect teacher. We are perfect New Creations, created in Christ Jesus.

We have perfect Righteousness. We have a perfect relationship. He says that we have become partakers of the very fulness of Christ.

"Of His fulness have we all received, and grace upon grace."

Our Redemption is perfect, completed Redemption that meets every need of the human and answers every challenge of divine fulness.

If this is true, I don't know why we cannot have complete knowledge. I want you to notice in Jn. 3:3-36 we are born "from Above."

The New Birth is not a work of psychology or of human philosophy or of human ability.

We are born "not of corruptible things but of incorruptible of the Word of God which liveth and abideth."

James tells us of His Own will He begat us.

Jn. 1:13, "We are born not of blood, nor of the will of the flesh nor of the will of man, but of God."

The New Creation is the work of the Holy Spirit through the Word. It is a perfect work.

It makes us complete in Him. "There is therefore now no condemnation to them that are in Christ Jesus." If you who read this can accept the Word, you will begin to blossom and bear fruit of joy and peace that you never knew.

We have been preached at so many years that we are poor, miserable creatures, that we are unworthy and unfit and the scriptures that were written to the Jews when they were in apostasy are applied to the church—also the scriptures to the unregenerate are applied to the church till the church has an inferiority complex in regard to sin.

It has lived in the realm of sin consciousness, and sense of unworthiness so long that the Word has little effect upon it.

We want to bring this to you today. The Word is a perfect message. You may have perfect knowledge of the Father's will.

It would be interesting to look up these scriptures.

Eph. 1:17, "That the God of our Lord Jesus Christ the Father of glory may give unto you a spirit of wisdom and Revelation in the Knowledge of Him."

It is not the knowledge of the Senses, but is the Knowledge of Him and the Spirit is going to guide your heart into this.

Eph. 4:13, "Till we all attain unto the unity of faith and the knowledge of the Son of God unto a full grown man, unto the measure of the stature of the fullness of Christ."

There is a complete and full knowledge to which we are going to grow.

This expression occurs 12 or 14 times in the New Testament, especially in the Epistles.

It has driven me to believe that the Father expects us to know His will.

Col. 1:12 (Rotherham's translation), "Giving thanks unto the Father who has given us the ability to enjoy our share of the inheritance of the saints in light."

The Greek word "dunamas" translated "power" means ability.

God has given us His ability to know His will to know what our share is in the inheritance of the saints in light.

We have the ability. It is God-given ability. We have the Holy Spirit whom Jesus said should guide us into all truth.

He is our teacher, our guide, our indwelling instructor. I cannot see where there is any ground for us to live in weakness and failure and ignorance of the Father's will and of our place and standing in Christ and of our rights and privileges.

We have no more right to dishonor the Father and dishonor Jesus than Jesus had when He walked here on earth.

We are the Sons and daughters of God. We are heirs of God and joint heirs with Jesus Christ.

We have privileges and rights in the family.

The first privilege is to make the heart of the Father glad.

Chapter Seventeen

HAVING YOUR OWN FAITH

Think of having faith in your own faith! Think of the thrill of having your own prayers answered!

A mother rushed up to me at the close of a service and said, "Oh, Mr. Kenyon, God heard my prayer last night and healed my baby."

She had been a Christian for years, and had never had her prayers answered.

A grandmother wrote, "You will never know the joy I have just experienced. My little grandchild was very ill, and in a dangerous condition. Then I remembered the Name of Jesus and my rights in Christ. I went into the sick room, knelt down by the baby, put my arms around it, and commanded in Jesus' Name that the disease leave and that the baby be healed. The mother stood by the bedside, tears streaming down her face. The baby opened his eyes, looked up at his mother and smiled. God had heard my prayer.

"I turned and laid my hands upon my daughter who had been sick ever since the child was born. She was healed.

"Can you imagine what this means to me? It is the first time in my life that I ever saw my prayers answered like that."

This should be the normal experience of everyone of you.

When you realize that the great majority of Christians

never have a prayer answered, you can understand what I mean by having your own faith.

Most Christians are depending upon other people's faith. They can do the praying, but they want someone else to do the believing.

In reality they are not praying. They are just repeating words, for prayer in the New Testament sense is born of faith, and is always answered.

The Father planned that all should have faith.

Have you noticed that passage of scriptures in Mark 16:17-18? "These signs shall accompany them that believe: in my name shall they cast out demons; they shall speak with new tongues; they shall take up serpents, and if they drink any deadly thing, it shall in no wise hurt them; they shall lay hands on the sick, and they shall recover."

Of whom is He speaking? Of the man or the woman who has just accepted Christ as Savior and confessed Him as Lord.

He has just received Eternal Life. At once he begins his combat with the unseen forces of darkness. Someone is sick or in bondage. He exercises his rights. In Jesus' Name he commands the power of Satan broken.

Acts 20:32 shows the place of the Word in the life of the believer. "Now I commend you to God, and to the word of his grace, which is able to build you up, and to give you the inheritance, among all them that are sanctified.

"To build you up" means to build you up in faith, in love, and in ability to help humanity.

Your faith may be developed until it becomes a mighty

force. That was the dream of the Father for you.

The Word will build up your sense of Righteousness. I know of nothing that is needed more than this.

When we become conscious that we are Righteous, we will not think of our weaknesses and failings.

Isaiah 32:17 "The work of righteousness shall be peace: and the effect of righteousness, quietness and confidence forever."

This verse does not belong to Israel. It is a prophecy of the Church.

The work of Righteousness that God wrought in you has brought peace to your heart.

Romans 8:1 "There is therefore now no condemnation to them that are in Christ Jesus."

You live in perfect quietness and rest.

The effect of Righteousness on your heart is a new quietness and a new type of faith.

You enjoy the effect of your confidence in the finished work of Christ.

You know that you are a master of circumstances.

You know that you are a master of demons.

You know that if you lay hands on a sick person, he will be healed.

The realization of this truth gives you a sense of quietness, a fulness of joy that you have never enjoyed before.

The phrase, "confidence forever," is striking. You have moved out of the restless atmosphere of fear and doubt, into the quiet waters of victory.

You have become a master where you served as a slave.

You are a conqueror where you suffered defeat.

You walk in the light where you walked in darkness.

You enjoy your privileges in Christ.

At last you have your own faith. At last you have arrived.

You know what John 15:5 means: "I am the vine; ye are the branches: He that abideth in me, and I in him, the same beareth much fruit: for apart from me ye can do nothing."

You enjoy the consciousness of the life of the vine abiding in you.

You are the fruit-bearing part of Christ.

You have been grafted into Him by the New Birth.

That graft has given you a new nature.

You bear the Jesus kind of fruit, which is love fruit, faith fruit.

The world is benefited by it. Christians are lifted everywhere you go into a new consciousness of their rights and privileges in Christ.

You know what John 15:7 means: "If ye abide in me, and my words abide in you, ask whatsoever ye will, and it shall be done unto you."

You know you do abide in Him. You bear the fruitage of His indwelling Word.

His Word in your lips produce real results.

The Father's Word in Jesus lips healed the sick. His Word in your lips does the same.

You know what it means to have legal rights, and

whatever you demand He gives you.

The word "demand" is used in its truest sense.

John 16:23-24 Jesus said, "In that day ye shall ask me nothing. Verily, verily, I say unto you, If ye shall ask anything of the Father, He will give it to you in my name."

The word "ask" means "demand."

It is not used in the sense that you command Him to give, but in the sense that you go into the bank and demand payment on your check. In the same sense your faith takes its rights, its portion.

At last you know what James 1:22-24 means.

"But be ye doers of the word, and not hearers only, deluding your own selves. For if anyone is a hearer of the word and not a doer, he is like unto a man beholding his natural face in a mirror: for he beholdeth himself, and goeth away, and straightway forgetteth what manner of man he was."

You have become a "doer of the Word." You are not just a hearer. You do not delude yourself with false hopes.

You are in Christ. You are an heir of God and a joint heir with Jesus Christ.

You know that His Word abides in you and produces results.

You are a producer. You are not marking time any longer.

You know now "what manner of man you are." You know that you are a New Creation, empowered by God.

The other day I looked at one of the new cars. The salesman said, "There is a 160 horsepower motor under that hood."

I said, "That could climb hills."

The man said, "It laughs at mountains."

I stood beside a believer. I said, "That man is empowered with God's ability. He laughs at all grades. He sings his song of triumph as he goes over in high. He is not a subject, a slave. He has passed out of that class into the class of a master.

He remembers in the morning what manner of man he is.

He faces life with a song of victory. The Word of Christ dwells in him richly in all wisdom and prudence. (Colossians 3:16).

The Word has become a part of God to him, a part of the living Christ to him.

Day by day the great, mighty Spirit who raised Jesus from the dead builds that Word into his spirit consciousness.

Christ is being formed in him.

One of these days, Christ, in all His fulness' will dominate him, until he will whisper softly, (Galatians 2:20) "It is no longer I that live, but Christ liveth in me.

Colossians 2:6-7 "As therefore ye received Christ Jesus as Lord, so walk in him, rooted and builded up in him, and established in your faith, even as ye were taught, abounding in thanksgiving."

The scripture is real to him.

Did you ever notice Ephesians 4:7? "But unto each one of us was the grace given, according to the measure of the gift of Christ?"

Now we are moving up into the big things.

The guide said, "In a few minutes we will be in the redwood section, and you will see the giants of the vegetable world."

I said softly as I walked into the prayer meeting, "We are coming into the spiritual redwoods. We are going to see spiritual giants, supermen. They have God dwelling in them. The Word of Christ is rich upon their lips. The love that relentlessly drove Jesus to the cross has gained possession of them.

"They no longer walk as natural men. They belong to the love class, the miracle class.

"They are in the Jesus class.

"They have graduated from the lower class.

"They are the men and women who have 'attained unto the unity of faith and the knowledge of the Son of God, and have become full-grown men unto the measure of the stature of the fulness of Christ.'

"They have their own faith. They are established in the truth. The Word is real to them."

Chapter Eighteen

LOVE'S IDENTIFICATION

We have seen that the New Creation is utterly one with Christ.

We have seen that the New Creation is one with Love, one with Him, and Love is one with the New Creation.

The new Creation is the body of Christ.

This living organism, God-dominated, God-filled, is here among men acting love, acting in His stead, taking over His work.

In the first chapter of Acts, Luke says by the Spirit, "The things Jesus began to do and teach."

We began where He left off.

We take up the work that He laid down

He was the Burden-Bearer, the Lover.

He is acting in us, through us, and with us.

BURDEN-BEARERS

We are now His burden-bearers.

We carry His load with His strength.

We do His will with His ability.

He is living His life in us.

We know, though perhaps we do not realize it that "It is no longer I that live, but Christ is living in me."

We have lost the old landmarks of Sense Knowledge since we learned to walk the new Way.

He said, "I am the way."

It is not a road; it is a person.

It is not a theory; it is a reality.

It is not a doctrine; it is a Life.

Dogma and Doctrines have lost their significance.

They are the worn-out shells of the yesterdays.

They held us in bondage for years.

Now we are swallowed up in Him.

Romans 15:1-2 "We that are strong ought to bear the infirmities of the weak, and not to please ourselves."

This is the Jesus method.

He was strong. He took our infirmities.

Now His strength has made us strong.

We take over the weaknesses of others.

We are not their critics.

We do not condemn them because they have failed.

We go down and take their burdens and let them walk by our side, freemen.

We do not condemn the one who is held in prison by Satan, for we remember that once we were slaves.

We are the strength-givers, the burden-bearers, the Light-leaders in the world of darkness.

What a ministry it is to take Jesus' place.

What a life it is to bear the burdens of the weak, carry the loads that others should have had strength to carry, have faith for those who are faithless, courage for those who are whipped, wisdom for those who have long walked in darkness.

We are the Jesus men and women of a new age.

John 15:9-10 "Even as the Father hath loved me, I also have loved you: abide ye in my love. If ye keep my commandments, ye shall abide in my love; even as I have kept my Father's commandments, and abide in his love."

We are to love as He loved, pour out our lives as He poured out His.

Paul saw the real issue and gave it to us in 2 Cor. 5:13-14 "For whether we are beside ourselves it is unto God; or whether we are of sober mind it is unto you. For the love of Christ constraineth us for we thus judge, that one died for all; therefore all died."

Paul believed in love to the extent that he was believed to be beside himself. Paul's answer was, "The love of Christ has taken hold of my heart. I realize that Christ's death was every man's death." The same love that caused Christ to die for man had constrained Paul's heart and was causing him to live for them.

The attitude of love is this, "I love them as though I had died for them." Paul is even stronger in his description of Love's identification in Romans 9:3 (Moffatt trans.) "I suffer endless anguish of heart. I could have wished myself accursed and banished from Christ for the sake of my brothers."

In reading this we feel we can hardly come up to it. But, it is not hard because He has made us Love. He has made us like Himself.

What He was in His earth walk, we are now in our earth walk.

He has taken us over in order that we might take over His dream for man.

It sounds strange, but it is beautifully true, that we love as He loved.

We love with His love.

We look upon people through love's eyes. We used to say, "They are reaping what they have sown." We used to see them through Sense-Knowledge eyes.

Now we say, "Father, help me to help them. I am taking your wisdom and your strength to carry the load that they have failed to take strength to carry. They have been deceived by Sense Knowledge. I take their place and carry their burden, as thou hast taken my place and borne my burden."

We speak of them with love's voice, with love's message.

LOVE'S TRANSMITTERS

Our Identification with Him put us on the throne.

His Identification with us puts us in the place of leaders, teachers, comforters, helpers, burden- bearers.

We bring God to man, just as He came to us.

We boldly say, "Look on us."

We are Love as He is Love. We are Love's lips, Love's hands and feet.

Without wires the mighty generator of Coulee Dam would be helpless.

Without transmitters, God in all His ability is helpless.

His love can find no expression except through the New Creation.

Those great generators are dependent on the wires. They, and they alone, can bear the current that can stir the motors and light the homes of the Northwest.

Can't you see if you fail Him, He is helpless?

We limit Him or we allow Him to be limitless.

For many ages the power and ability of the mighty Columbia was never utilized.

For nearly two thousand years the limitless ability of God has been unused.

The church has been weak and powerless.

Sin has reigned as a master, and the church has served as a slave.

Yet that church represents the New Creation which is a Satan-conqueror.

Shall we allow it to go on?

You have seen the truth in this mighty message of Identification.

What are you going to do with it?

WE HOLD THE KEY

Shall God be great among men once more?

Shall He heal and save the multitudes?

Shall the vast hordes of men once more hear the message of grace from lips set on fire with love?

Shall the Peters once more walk the waves?

Shall we hear them say to the crippled, "Arise, walk."

Shall we see men set free from Satan's dominion?

Yes, I believe we shall.

We are the masters.

We have arrived.

We have the thing the human spirit has craved.

We are whispering now, "Greater is He who is in us, than any opposition or any lack that may confront us."

Can't you hear a voice saying, "This is God speaking?"

We remember what manner of men and women He has made us.

We fear not.

At last we are masters.

We are the God-created, the God-indwelt, the God-empowered, the God-guided.

We are the ones in whom love never faileth.

Come, let us go up and take the land! We are well able!

CONCLUSION

When these truths really gain the ascendancy in us, they will make us spiritual supermen, masters of demons and diseases.

This is an unveiling of what we are in Christ, how the Father sees us in the Son.

It will be the end of weakness and failure. There will be no more struggle for faith, for all things are ours. There will be no more praying for power, for He is in us. There will no longer be the awful bondage of sin consciousness, for we are the Righteousness of God in Christ.

We know what we are in Christ.

We know that He dwells in us.

We know the authority of His Name.

We are God-inside minded.

We have His ability.

We have His wisdom.

We have His love.

We are His Righteousness.

He lives in us.

His lordship is a reality.

His Word is present-tense to our hearts.

We have a standing invitation to His throne room.

We are invited to come boldly into His presence.

We are seated with Him in Heaven.

He is with us on Earth.

In the presence of these tremendous realities we arise and take our place. We go out and live as supermen indwelt of God.

IDENTIFIED

1. In crucifixion on the cross,
     With Jesus Christ identified;
   In death for man's eternal loss,
     With Jesus Christ identified.

Chorus
   Identified, identified,
     With Jesus Christ identified;
   In all He was, or is, or shall be.
   Eternally identified.

2. In burial 'neath the cursed ground,
     With Jesus Christ identified;
   In Hell's deep dungeons where He's found,
     With Jesus Christ identified.

3. In vict'ry over hells dark host,
     With Jesus Christ identified;
   Yes, while He paid sin's awful cost,
     With Jesus Christ identified.

4. In resurrection might and pow'r,
     With Jesus Christ identified;
   At God's right hand this very hour,
     With Jesus Christ identified.

5. In coronation's glorious day,
     ' With Jesus Christ identified;
   When He by right shall kingdoms sway,
     With Jesus Christ identified.

—E.W.K.

Inspiring Books by E. W. KENYON

THE BIBLE in the light of Our Redemption
    A Basic Bible Course

ADVANCED BIBLE COURSE
    Studies in the Deeper Life

THE HIDDEN MAN of the Heart

WHAT HAPPENED
    From the Cross to the Throne

NEW CREATIONS REALITIES

IN HIS PRESENCE
    The Secret of Prayer

THE TWO KINDS OF LIFE

THE FATHER AND HIS FAMILY
    The Story of Man's Redemption

THE WONDERFUL NAME OF JESUS
    Our Rights and Privileges in Prayer

JESUS THE HEALER
    Has Brought Healing to Thousands

KENYON'S LIVING POEMS

THE NEW KIND OF LOVE

THE TWO KINDS OF FAITH

THE TWO KINDS OF RIGHTEOUSNESS

THE BLOOD COVENANT

THE TWO KINDS OF KNOWLEDGE

SIGN POSTS ON THE ROAD TO SUCCESS

IDENTIFICATION

Order From:
KENYON'S GOSPEL PUBLISHING SOCIETY
P.O. Box 973, Lynnwood Washington 98046-0973
Website: www.kenyons.org